Typing Tutor III™ with Letter Invaders™ for the Entire IBM PC Family: PC, XT, AT, and PCjr

by Kriya Systems, Inc.

Simon & Schuster, Inc.
New York

Published by the Computer Software Division
Simon & Schuster, Inc.

Simon & Schuster Building
Rockefeller Center
1230 Avenue of the Americas
New York, New York 10020

SIMON AND SCHUSTER and colophon are registered trademarks of Simon & Schuster, Inc.

Typing Tutor III, Letter Invaders, Time Response Monitoring, TRM, and Kriya Systems are trademarks owned by, and licensed from, Kriya Systems, Inc.

IBM PC, PC/XT, PC AT, and PCjr are registered trademarks of the International Business Machines Corporation. This book is not authorized by the International Business Machines Corporation.

Designed by Stanley S. Drate/Folio Graphics Co., Inc.

Manufactured in the United States of America

Printed and bound by Kingsport Press

10 9 8 7 6 5

ISBN: 0-671-30906-4

Contents

Welcome to the Typing Tutor III Software Package with the Letter Invaders Game

The Typing Tutor III keyboard-instruction program is a unique system that can teach you to type faster, more efficiently, and more enjoyably than any book or class. It is composed of a series of typing lessons and tests that are continually adjusted to your proficiency level. Even if you have never used a keyboard before, this program will have you typing with ease and confidence in a very short time.

You'll start off with just a few keys. When you can type these keys easily, the Typing Tutor III program adds a few more, creating custom-designed lessons especially for you. Using these lessons, you will quickly learn to type the alphabet, special symbols, and numbers accurately and easily. If you have an IBM PC, XT, or AT and do a lot of calculations on the computer, you may also want to work on lessons that teach the numeric keypad.

How does this software work its magic? Simple. The program notes the time it takes you to type each letter, then uses this information to create each new lesson for you. This process is called Time Response Monitoring™, or TRM™. Thanks to the TRM process, the Typing Tutor III program doesn't bore you with drills on keys you've already learned or make you anxious with lessons that are too difficult. Instead, it creates lessons and practice tests that encourage you to respond automatically and without errors, because they are specifically tailored to your own unique requirements.

No Typing Manual

The only pages requiring your attention are the few you are looking at right now. The purpose of this booklet is to give you an idea of what the Typing Tutor III program is all about, and to help you get started. Everything else you may need is on the diskette, a mere keystroke away. You'll find this electronic documentation infinitely more convenient than searching through a manual. You won't get bogged down with odds and ends that you don't need and didn't ask for. If you find yourself unsure of something, just press the question-mark key and you'll have your answer. This "Help" feature is available from all screens that display a question mark in the bottom left corner.

In addition to the Help screens located throughout the program, the electronic documentation includes a series of introductory screens to give you an overview of features and capabilities. Once you get the program loaded into your computer, the Introduction is immediately available. We will go through the procedure for loading the program and getting started. First, however, there are a few pointers you should know, especially if you are new to computers.

Removal and Care of the Diskette

To remove the diskette from the plastic envelope (*after* you have read the End User License Agreement in the back of this book), use scissors or a sharp knife to cut the seal of the envelope's top horizontal edge. When not using the diskette, return it to this envelope for safekeeping. The diskette is magnetic and should be handled carefully. Placing it on or

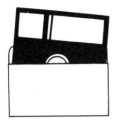

Store Properly

Don't bend

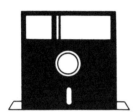

Insert Carefully

Don't touch
exposed surface

Store at
10°C-53°C
50°F-125°F

Keep away from
magnetic fields

near anything magnetic could erase information. Objects such as loudspeakers, kitchen appliances, and paper clip holders all apply! And let's not commit the most common crime against diskettes, which is leaving them on a computer or monitor. These may seem like convenient places for a diskette, but in fact, damage to the diskette may result. Also, do not touch the surface of the diskette itself (the platter inside the protective sleeve), and avoid bending it or subjecting it to temperature extremes.

10

Making a Backup Copy

Copy me first...

Even though you plan to take good care of your software, accidents do happen. Therefore, you would be wise to make a backup copy of the Typing Tutor III program diskette and store the original in a safe place.

... but not more than once.

Please understand that copying this program to sell or give to anyone else is against the law. This includes distribution within schools and clubs.

If you wish to begin the program without first making a backup copy of the Typing Tutor III diskette, skip down to the section Loading the Program Without Making a Backup Copy.

NOTE: If you are using a system with single-sided disk drives rather than the prevalent double-sided drives, watch for the double asterisks (**) during the diskette copying and loading procedures. Single-sided drive systems require special consideration in some of the following steps owing to insufficient memory space on single-sided diskettes. This lack of space does not affect the Typing Tutor III program; it only means that DOS (the disk operating system) cannot be present on the same diskette. Comments preceded by asterisks will keep you on track. If your system has double-sided drives, ignore the asterisked comments.

The chart below outlines the commands necessary to make your backup copy. These commands differ among the four types of disk-drive configurations. If this is your first time making a backup diskette, please read the instructions, using the chart as a point of reference. If you are familiar with the process but just want to confirm which commands to use while following screen prompts, the chart may be all you'll need.

System	Format Command	Copy Command
2 double-sided disk drives	format b:/s	copy *.* b:
2 single-sided disk drives	–	diskcopy a: b:
1 double-sided disk drive*	–	diskcopy
1 single-sided disk drive	–	diskcopy

*Usually the PCjr and the PC AT have this configuration.

NOTE: The Typing Tutor III program diskette has the PC, XT, and AT versions on one side and the PCjr version on the other. The program on the PC side of the diskette uses an advanced technology that automatically determines whether the computer is a PC, an AT, or an XT and adjusts itself accordingly. When making the backup copy, be sure to insert the program diskette into the drive with the appropriate side facing up.

To copy with two disk drives:

1. Insert your PC DOS diskette into drive A (the one on the left), close the drive door, and turn on the computer. If requested, enter the date and time, or press RETURN twice to skip these prompts. (Whenever you see the word RETURN in the Typing Tutor III electronic documentation, remember that it refers to the ↵ or Enter key on your computer.) A moment later an "A>" will appear on the screen, indicating that you are in DOS.

2. For double-sided drives, format a blank diskette and transfer DOS to it by typing **format b:/s** and pressing RETURN. Insert a blank diskette into drive B (the drive on the right) in response to the request on the screen. Close the drive door. Press RETURN and wait until the computer finishes formatting the diskette (the "in use" light will go off). Type **n** to indicate that you do not want to format another diskette.

    **For single-sided drives, skip to the asterisked note under step 3.

3. Insert the Typing Tutor III program diskette into drive A. Your newly formatted diskette remains in drive B. Then type **copy *.* b:** and press RETURN. When the "A>" appears, the copy is complete.

    For single-sided drives, leave DOS in drive A, type **diskcopy a: b: and press RETURN. As prompted, remove the DOS diskette and insert the Typing Tutor III program diskette (the *source* diskette, i.e., the one to be copied) into drive A, the newly formatted *target* diskette (the backup diskette) into drive B, and press any key. In a moment the message "Copy complete—Copy another (Y/N)?" will appear. Type **n,** for no, to indicate that you do not wish to make any more copies.

4. Remove your backup copy of the Typing Tutor III program from drive B and label it with the label provided. Store the original in a safe place.

5. To load the program, insert your backup diskette into drive A, and simultaneously press the Ctrl, Alt, and Del keys. (Or you can turn the computer off, then on again.)

    **To load the program, insert the DOS diskette into drive A and press Ctrl, Alt, and Del simultaneously. Once the "A>" prompt appears, remove DOS from the drive and insert the Typing Tutor

III backup diskette. Type **TT** and press RETURN. The program will load into the computer's memory and display the opening menu.

To copy with one disk drive:

1. Insert your PC DOS diskette into drive A, close the drive door, and turn on the computer. If requested, enter the time and date, or press RETURN twice to skip these prompts. (Whenever you see the word RETURN in the Typing Tutor III electronic documentation, remember that it refers to the ↵ or Enter key on your computer.) An "A>" will appear on the screen, indicating you are in DOS.
2. Type **diskcopy** and press RETURN. You'll see the message:

> Insert source diskette in drive A:
> Strike any key when ready.

Remove DOS from the drive, insert the Typing Tutor III program diskette, and press any key. Because you do not have a second drive, you will have to switch diskettes a few times. Whenever you see a reference to the *target* diskette during the copying procedure, put the backup diskette into the drive. *Source* diskette refers to the Typing Tutor III program diskette.

NOTE: Copying a diskette with a single drive on the PC AT requires that the target diskette *not* be a 1.2-megabyte, high-density, 96-tracks-per-inch diskette. Use a single- or double-sided, double-density, 40-track diskette as the target diskette.
3. Press any key to tell DOS that you have switched diskettes. The computer will put the Typing Tutor III program information it reads from the

original diskette onto the backup copy. Messages will tell you to swap diskettes a few times, until the message "Copy complete—Copy another (Y/N)?" appears. Insert the DOS diskette and type **n** to indicate that you do not wish to make any more copies. The "A>" prompt will be displayed. Put the provided label on the backup diskette.

4. To load the program, insert the Typing Tutor III backup diskette into the drive. Type **TT** and press RETURN. Once the program is loaded, it will display the opening menu.

The single-sided and/or single-drive backup diskettes do not contain DOS. Therefore, the PC DOS diskette must be in the drive when you turn on the computer or when you use the Ctrl-Alt-Del method of restarting the system. Then, replace the DOS diskette with the Typing Tutor III backup diskette, type **TT** at the "A>" prompt, and press RETURN.

Loading the Program Without Making a Backup Copy

To load the Typing Tutor III program without first copying it, follow these steps:

1. Load PC DOS into your computer (if it isn't there already) by inserting your DOS diskette into drive A (the drive on the left) and turning on the computer. If the computer asks for the date and time, you can respond by typing in these values, or press RETURN twice to skip these prompts. (Whenever you see the word RETURN in Typing Tutor III electronic documentation, remember

that it refers to the ⏎ or Enter key on your computer.) The "A>" tells you that you are in DOS.

2. Now remove the DOS diskette from drive A and insert the Typing Tutor III program diskette with the appropriate side facing up. (One side of the program diskette has the PC, XT, and AT versions and the other side has the PCjr version.) Type **TT** beside the drive prompt (A>) and press RETURN. Or, if you have two disk drives and would like to keep DOS in drive A and load the Typing Tutor III program from drive B, type **B:** and press RE-TURN. This switches the logged drive from A to B. Then type **TT** beside the drive prompt (B>) and press RETURN. The opening menu will be displayed.

If You Have a PCjr, Read This!

The screens illustrated in this book are from the IBM PC, XT, and AT versions of the Typing Tutor III program, so they'll look a little different from the PCjr screens. Don't be concerned! The information on the screens is essentially the same, but because the PC, XT, and AT have 80 columns of characters displayed on their screens and the PCjr has 40, the PCjr screens are a bit less wordy. Be assured that PCjr screens say and do all they need to!

Getting Started

Once you have loaded the Typing Tutor III program, the computer will display the opening *menu* (a screen on which a selection is made). The first option, BEGIN PROGRAM, is the entrance to the les-

TYPING TUTOR III (TM) with LETTER INVADERS (TM)

Press the space bar to see how it moves the cursor (the diamond pointer) between the items in this menu. All menus in the Typing Tutor III program work this way. Move to the option of your choice by pressing the space bar, then press RETURN to make your selection. If this is your first time with this software, or you need to refresh your memory, choose READ INTRODUCTION for information. If you are ready to begin, select BEGIN PROGRAM to advance to the main program menu.

```
    ♦ BEGIN PROGRAM
      READ INTRODUCTION
```

Published by the Electronic Publishing Division of Simon & Schuster, Inc.

Press RETURN to begin the Typing Tutor III program.

sons, tests, and game that are featured in this program. The second option, READ INTRODUCTION, will display a series of screens describing the various aspects of the program, how they work, and how they interact to produce optimum results.

Ready for the tour? Let's start by pressing the space bar (the long bar at the bottom of the keyboard). Notice that the cursor (the little diamond on the screen) jumps from option to option. The space bar functions this way on all menus. Each time you press it, the cursor moves to the next option, and a message at the bottom of the screen states what will happen if you press RETURN to choose that option.

Move the cursor to READ INTRODUCTION and press RETURN. This brings you to the first of a

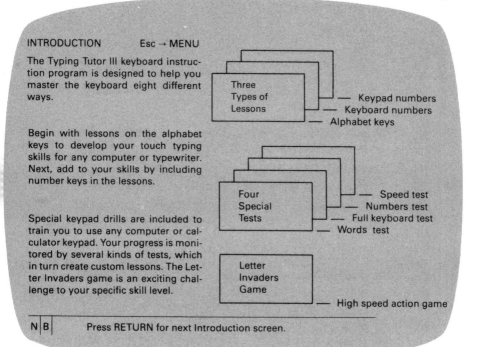

INTRODUCTION   Esc → MENU

The Typing Tutor III keyboard instruction program is designed to help you master the keyboard eight different ways.

Begin with lessons on the alphabet keys to develop your touch typing skills for any computer or typewriter. Next, add to your skills by including number keys in the lessons.

Special keypad drills are included to train you to use any computer or calculator keypad. Your progress is monitored by several kinds of tests, which in turn create custom lessons. The Letter Invaders game is an exciting challenge to your specific skill level.

Three Types of Lessons — Keypad numbers — Keyboard numbers — Alphabet keys

Four Special Tests — Speed test — Numbers test — Full keyboard test — Words test

Letter Invaders Game — High speed action game

N B   Press RETURN for next Introduction screen.

series of screens that tell you what the Typing Tutor III program is about. These screens offer a general overview; more specific information comes from the Help screens, available throughout the program.

Take a look at the various parts of this introductory screen. Since all screens in the program have similar layouts, it will help you to know what to look for on each one. In the top left corner is the name of the screen. Most screens also display an escape message at the top, indicating that pressing the Esc key will take you a step back in the program. From this screen, pressing Esc will return you to the opening menu. The escape function is explained in detail later in the Introduction.

The bulk of the display is information. At the

bottom of the screen is a line, with an "N" and a "B" just below it in the left corner. The cursor is over the N when the screen first comes up. Press the space bar now and see that, just as in a menu, it moves the cursor to B and back again, and the message along the bottom line changes simultaneously. You can press the space bar as often as you like; all it does is show you your options.

The N and B will appear when you have a series of related screens, such as the Introduction screens and some of the Help screens (where there is more information than can fit on a single screen). The *N* stands for *next,* and if you press RETURN with the cursor on N, you will proceed to the next screen of the series. The *B* means *back* or *before,* and selecting it will take you out of the Introduction or Help screens to the menu from which you originally requested information.

Press RETURN with the cursor at N and proceed to the next Introduction screen. Now relax and experiment a bit. Press Esc and see the same screen you just came from. Select N again and return to the second Introduction screen. Press RETURN and see the third screen of the Introduction series. Select B and jump back to the opening menu. Select READ INTRODUCTION again and read through the entire set of Introduction screens, and you will have an idea of what lies ahead as you work with this program. After the Introduction sequence has been completed, the program will automatically loop back to the opening menu. When this happens, you are ready for the next portion of this tour.

You should now have on your screen the opening menu once again. This time, press RETURN with the cursor beside the option BEGIN PROGRAM. Screens for you to type in your name will appear. This is to establish a file for yourself in the program, which will then keep track of your progress. You can either enter your name and begin your own history file, or just press RETURN and work "anonymously." For the purpose of this walk-through, you needn't enter your name. But then again, if you want to, go right ahead! Press RETURN to proceed to the program's main menu.

The Main Menu

At this point you should be looking at the screen containing ten options (nine in the PCjr version), beginning with ALPHABET KEYS. This is the main Typing Tutor III program menu, from which you can choose a variety of lessons and tests, and even play a

---

MAIN MENU

Alphabet or number drills help you learn the keys. Tests measure your progress and create lessons. The Letter Invaders (TM) game is a fast-action challenge to your skills. Status is where you may adjust flexible program conditions. The Introduction is a series of screens that provide an overview of the program. For more information on these features, press the space bar until you reach INTRODUCTION, then press RETURN.

```
  ◆ ALPHABET KEYS
    KEYBOARD NUMBERS
    KEYPAD NUMBERS
    WORDS TEST
    FULL KEYBOARD TEST
    NUMBERS TEST
    STANDARD SPEED TEST
    LETTER INVADERS GAME
    STATUS REPORT
    INTRODUCTION
```

? |M|G|Q| Begin here to practice the alphabet keys.

great game. The Introduction is also available from this menu, for convenience.

As always, the space bar moves the cursor from option to option. (Go ahead, try it!) The messages briefly describe what each option is about. The four symbols in the bottom left corner are also reached by the cursor. These options may be accessed either by typing the characters directly from the keyboard or by spacing to them and pressing RETURN.

Whenever you see a question mark in that corner, you can position the cursor on it and press RETURN, or just press the question-mark key, and a Help message will be displayed. If you do so now (please do), you'll get information about the menu. If this screen looks familiar to you, it's because the Help for the main menu is identical to the first few Introduction screens (in the PC, XT, and AT versions only). Combining these two screens saved valuable memory space by avoiding a repetition of information. (No other Help screens are repeated elsewhere.) Select N if you would like to advance to the next Introduction screen. If you do not want to proceed through the Introduction (which will ultimately cycle back to the menu), select B to return to the menu instantly.

The letters *MGQ* beside the question mark at the bottom stand for *menu, graph,* and *quit,* as you can see if you space down to these options and read the corresponding messages. All of these are explained in the Introduction, so we won't go into them here. The purpose of this tour is to help you understand that everything you need is readily available within the program. Messages are always displayed to keep you informed and on the right track. You have great mobility throughout the whole program; the more you venture into the various areas, the more you'll find and the more you'll gain.

The Lessons

Before you get involved with your own typing work, please invest a few more minutes in our Typing Tutor III program tour. Doing so will help clarify a few things that otherwise may escape your notice. From the main menu, select ALPHABET KEYS by pressing RETURN with the cursor beside the first option. You should now have the Alphabet Keys lesson displayed on your screen. This display may appear to be self-explanatory, but let's take a look anyway, to be on the safe side.

In the top left corner is the title announcing what the screen is all about. To the right of the title is the message telling you that pressing Esc will take you from the lesson to the Progress Report. This is an option you may take if you do not want to complete a lesson set and would rather pull out. If you complete the set, the program automatically advances to a report of your progress.

The next item on the screen is the set of keys to be typed in this lesson. The keys to type in the first lesson (for a new "student") are the home keys **ASDF**. These are the home keys for the left hand, where your fingers remain stationed on the keyboard. From these keys (**ASDF** for the left hand and **JKL;** for the right) you can comfortably and methodically reach all the others. The diagram on page 22 illustrates how correct fingering works on the keyboard (and keypad on the PC, XT, and AT.)

Notice how the keyboard is divided into areas. Each finger is responsible for the keys in its area. The index fingers cover the areas numbered 1; the middle fingers cover the number 2 areas; ring fingers work the keys in the areas numbered 3; and little fingers cover the keys in the areas numbered 4. The space bar works easily with the thumbs. The SHIFT

IBM PC and XT Keyboard*

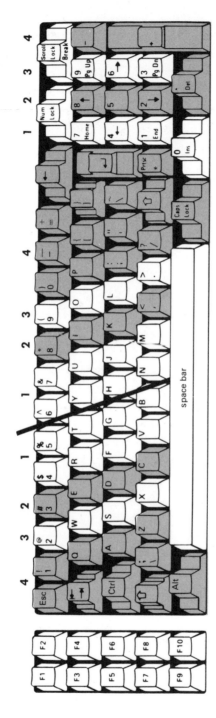

Fingering is as follows: 1 = index, 2 = middle, 3 = ring, 4 = little finger. Use thumb for space bar and for 0 on keypad.

*Though the PC AT keyboard looks a little different and the PCjr keyboard has no numeric keypad, the fingering for both is the same as shown above.

keys (the two keys on either side of the keyboard that are marked with large upward-pointing arrows) should be pressed with the little finger of the hand that is not making the keystroke. Remember to keep your fingers oriented on the home keys, and the locations of all other keys will soon be found by automatic response.

Take another look at the Alphabet Keys lesson on your screen. The Speed and Errors section will be blank until you have given the program something to calculate. Lower on the screen is a diagram of the keyboard, which is your guide to successful learning. It works like this. As you type the two sets of four keys that are displayed, you should *not* watch your fingers. Instead, place your fingers on the home keys before you begin and keep your eyes on the screen when you type. This is an important point to remember.

On the screen's keyboard, the letters to practice in that specific lesson are the only letters identified. Their placement on the board is clear, and once your fingers are established on the home keys, you'll have no problem finding them by following the diagram *on the screen*, not the actual keyboard. The intention here is to keep your eyes off your hands; otherwise, you will nurture the habit of watching the keyboard and may never learn by heart the location of the keys. Successful typing is dependent on knowing the keyboard and getting around it by feel, not by sight.

The Progress Report

Leave the lesson now by pressing Esc. The Progress Report comes up, although it will have no speed or accuracy data to report (unless you couldn't resist and typed the lesson). If you take a lesson and consistently type keys with speed and accuracy, those keys will be shown on the keyboard display in reversed video, proclaiming them "fast." For more information on progress, press the question-mark key. Once you see the progress Help screens and have returned to the Progress Report, press **M** to display the main menu once again.

Leaving the Typing Tutor III Program

When you are ready to quit using the program, press Esc to get to a screen with ?MGQ options in the lower left corner. (If the screen already has these prompts, there is no need to press Esc.) Press **Q**, or move the cursor to Q and press RETURN. If your name is on file with the program, you have two choices at this point: RECORD PROGRESS or END PROGRAM.

RECORD PROGRESS adds to your history file the results of the lessons and tests you have taken during this session. This file will keep an ongoing record of your work as long as you begin each session by identifying yourself. After pressing RETURN to record your progress, the program will take you out to the "A>" or "B>" prompt, where you can load other software, turn off your computer, or reload the Typing Tutor III program by typing **TT** and pressing RETURN.

If you do not wish to record your progress, or did not identify yourself at the beginning of this session, use the END PROGRAM option to leave the program and return to the "A>" or "B>" prompt.

You're on Your Own

Are you getting the picture? There are lessons for the letter keys, the numbers along the top of the keyboard, and the numbers on the keypad (except in the PCjr version). There are four types of tests for you to try, which in turn will present Test Results. Help screens are available everywhere.

NOTE: As much on-screen help as possible is present in the PCjr version; however, Appendix A has been added to this book to supplement the jr's Help system. Due to less available memory in the computer, the entire Help network could not be implemented on-screen.

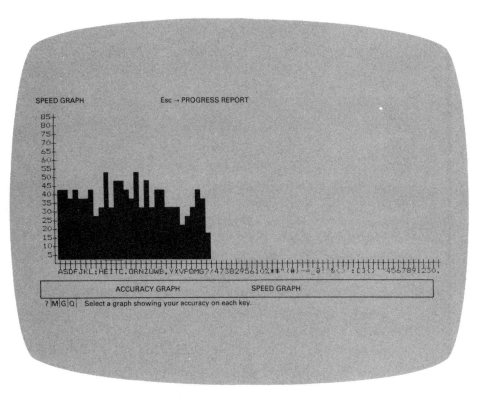

Graphs are available to illustrate for you how you are doing; you can see these from any screen displaying the four characters (?MGQ) in the bottom left corner by pressing RETURN with the cursor over the G or by pressing the **G** key. A speed graph is displayed automatically as part of the quit sequence when you exit the program.

Select STATUS REPORT from the main menu if you would like to see what properties in the program may be changed, and then change them if you like, following the instructions in the associated Help screen.

By now, you should have an idea of what the Typing Tutor III program is about. By experimenting with the menus and Help screens and lessons, you should have a basic grasp on how to get around to the other features which are not discussed on these pages. Never be hesitant to explore.

The Letter Invaders™ Game

Caution: This game may be habit forming! The excitement generated by blasting letters that zoom down from outer space while keeping correct finger placement on the keyboard cannot be justly described; it can only be experienced. The Letter Invaders™ game provides a great break from the usual typing drills. Select the game from the main menu when you dare.

NOTE: The running score appears only on the PC, XT, and AT versions. On all versions the scorecard is displayed when the game ends.

Letters: 106   Hits: 93   ASDFJKL;HEITC.ORNZUWB,ZXVPQMG?/4738295610

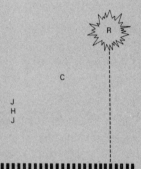

Parting Words

Just a few parting comments on the art of working with the Typing Tutor III program, to ensure that you'll get off on the right foot.

- Always watch the screen, not your hands.
- Keep your fingers on the home keys. The home keys are **ASDF JKL;** on the keyboard and **456** on the IBM PC keypads. The plus key (+) to the right of the IBM PC, XT, or AT keypad functions as the RETURN for the pads.

- The NUMBERS TEST selected from the main menu tests you on the IBM PC keypad if you have most recently worked with the keypad. Otherwise, a test on numbers will be a keyboard numbers test, requiring you to press the space bar between groups of numbers and RETURN (rather than the plus key) at the end of each line. On the PCjr, a test on numbers will always be a keyboard numbers test.

- The keys with large up-arrows on either side of the keyboard are the SHIFT keys. Pressing either one converts lowercase to uppercase on alphabetic keys and gives access to the top symbols on other keys. Shifting should be done with the little finger of the hand that is not making the keystroke.

- After a lesson, a Progress Report is displayed. After a test, a Test Results screen is displayed. After a game, a Scorecard is displayed.

- The Esc key will back you out of your current position or, in the event of being in the middle of a lesson, test, or game, will take you to the progress, results, or scorecard screen. Where Esc will take you is printed on the top of each "escape active" screen.

- You can switch students by exiting the program and reentering with the next student's name. To exit the program, select the Q (quit) option on the screen (first press the Esc key if the ?MGQ options are not currently available in the lower left corner). If you entered your name when you started the program, you will then be given a chance to store a permanent record of your Progress Report. Once you have the "A>" or "B>" prompt on the screen, you can reenter the program by typing **TT** and pressing RETURN. Then take the BEGIN PRO-GRAM option, and the screen that requests a name will appear, at which time you can type (or choose) the next student's name.

- It is possible to get printed copies of Typing Tutor III screens by pressing the SHIFT and PrtSc keys simultaneously. (Of course, you need a printer.) The printer may not understand some of the graphics characters that are displayed on screens containing boxes or other art. This could result in odd characters on paper where normal graphics appear on the screen. Keyboard letters, numbers, and symbols should print with no problem.

Onward

You are now ready to begin typing. If you would like the program to pinpoint your weak areas, begin by selecting WORDS TEST from the main menu and taking a few tests. Otherwise, the place to begin is the Alphabet Keys drill (which you can also select from the main menu, remember?). Carry on at your own pace and enjoy the experience you'll have with the Typing Tutor III program that wouldn't be possible with a book and typewriter. Learning a new skill could hardly be more pleasant.

Appendix A: PCjr Version Supplementary Information on the Main Menu, Progress Reports, and Test Results

This appendix has been prepared to supplement the electronic documentation in areas where explanation exceeds available space in the program.

The Main Menu

At the main menu, select from lessons, tests, the Letter Invaders game, program status, or the Introduction.

ALPHABET KEYS is the place to begin if you want to get acquainted with the keyboard. These lessons start out on the "home" keys (**ASDF JKL;**) where your fingers generally rest while typing. As soon as you learn these keys, the program will show each of the other keys in combination with a home key to help you learn the complete keyboard.

KEYBOARD NUMBERS is the next skill to add. These lessons introduce each number key in the top row of the keyboard in combination with one of the home keys. This helps you use correct fingering for fast, accurate typing of all numbers.

WORDS TEST can be selected from the main menu or from the lessons. If selected from the main menu, the words will be made up of all letters. If a words test is selected following a lesson (from the Progress Report screen), only the keys you've worked on are used in the test.

FULL KEYBOARD TEST helps experienced typists increase speed and accuracy in a single practice session. This test discovers the specific keys that block fast, accurate typing. Subsequent lessons concentrate on these keys and rapidly improve performance.

NUMBERS TEST checks your ability with the keyboard numbers. The results create lessons to help you improve in your weak areas. If you select this test from the main menu, all numbers are included. If you choose this option following a lesson, only the numbers you've been working on are included.

STANDARD SPEED TEST shows how your speed and accuracy would be measured on a standard typing test. The typing speed figures are adjusted to compensate for errors.

The LETTER INVADERS fast-action video game improves your typing as you defend your planet against invading fleets from outer space.

In STATUS REPORT you can change program variables, if you wish. These options are generally not changed, but you are offered the chance to turn the sound on or off, change the threshold at which the response time for a key is considered fast by the program, change the number of lessons that are presented by the program before a Progress Report is displayed (from 1 to 100 lessons), and alter the number of lines contained in a test (from 1 to 7 lines).

Progress Report

Keyboard Display

This display shows your progress in mastering each key. Those keys typed faster than the words per minute figure at the top of the display are shown in reverse and are considered to be "fast."

The speed at which a key is considered fast is adjustable. At the onset, the wpm is set at 20 words per minute. This speed may be increased, requiring faster typing before a key is considered fast, or it may be reduced with the opposite effect. This adjustment is made from either the Progress Report or the Status Report.

Performance Data

After ten lesson sets, the details of your performance are displayed. Shown in the working keys category are keys being used to create your lessons. These keys must be typed faster than the wpm figure shown above the keyboard display and with at least 80% accuracy, at which point they are considered learned.

NOTE: You may make an adjustment on the Status Report screen to alter the number of sets to be completed before a Progress Report screen is shown. You can arrange to type anywhere from 1 to 100 lesson sets between Progress Reports, if you wish. The program will display 10 sets before a report is shown unless it is changed.

The actual speed is your typing speed with no adjustment for error. The corrected speed subtracts five words per minute from the actual speed for each mistake.

The accuracy indicates how much of your work is correct. If your accuracy is low, consider choosing the option to build more speed from your Progress Report screen. This will cause the program to delay adding more letters to the drills until the current set is typed with higher proficiency.

Progress Report Menu

At the conclusion of the report, this menu offers four choices. If you select the first option, the lessons will continue as they have been. Pressing RETURN after each Progress Report will automatically continue the lessons.

If you choose to build more speed, the words per minute speed required for a key to be considered fast will be raised by 10 percent, so new keys will not be introduced until present keys are typed at a faster pace. In the option to learn more keys, the wpm is lowered by 10 percent so new keys are introduced more often.

If you would like to test your progress, the last option on the Progress Report screen will create a words test made up of letters you are learning. After this test you may continue these lessons or use the test results to create new lessons that build speed and accuracy on your slower keys.

Test Results

Keyboard Display

This display shows your progress in mastering each key. Those keys typed faster than the words per minute figure at the top of the display are shown in reverse.

The speed at which a key is considered fast is adjustable. When you start the program, the speed is set at 20 words per minute. This speed may be increased, requiring faster typing speed before a key is considered fast, or it may be reduced with the opposite effect. This adjustment is made from either the Progress Report or the Status Report.

Performance Data

Your performance is rated in terms of keys you mistyped, your actual speed (with no adjustment for mistakes), your corrected speed (subtracting 5 wpm for each error), and your accuracy percentage.

Test Results Menu

The Test Results screen also has a menu offering three choices. If you choose to create new lessons, the program will build a series of lessons based on the results of this test. These lessons emphasize the keys that you type more slowly and assist you in building your speed and accuracy.

If you repeat the same test, the results will accumulate. This creates more information about your typing speed and accuracy on each key and allows the program to build lessons that closely match your learning curve.

The option to continue lessons allows you to build a series of lessons without using the results of the test just completed. If you have completed one or more lessons and feel that they represent your skills better than this test, select this option. The program will then return to the lesson with no change. The results of this test will not be acknowledged by the program if the option to continue lessons is selected.

Appendix B: Incorporating Your Own Speed Test into the Typing Tutor III Program

The Typing Tutor III program has a variety of tests, but it contains only one speed test, the Standard Speed Test, which is comparable to many standard typing tests. If you find yourself becoming familiar with the Standard Speed Test to the extent that you no longer find it a challenge to your skills, there is a way to put a test of new words and sentences of your choice into the program. This appendix describes how this may be done.

The Standard Speed Test is recognized by the program as a disk file named STDTST.001 (an abbreviation of *standard test*). Each screen in the Typing Tutor III program is actually a disk file, displayed by the program at the appropriate time.

The best way to replace the standard test with your own is to rename the original test and record your test onto the diskette using STDTST.001 as its name. The active test *must* have this name because it is the filename the program will look for when STANDARD SPEED TEST is selected from the menu. We suggest saving the original test in case you would like to reactivate it in the future. As long as it is filed under a new name, it can be on the Typing Tutor III program diskette as an inactive file.

To replace our test with yours, you need to know how text editing works on your computer. You may use a word processing program or the line editor that comes on a DOS diskette. Since there are countless editing possibilities, it would be impractical to attempt to cover them all here.

The guidelines for writing a new test are:

1. In DOS, rename the original test file. The name STDTST.002 would work and would be easy to recall later. Renaming is done with the command **rename STDTST.001, STDTST.002**.

2. The new test should not exceed seven lines in length. Fifty-two characters are the most that should be on a line. Characters beyond these boundaries will be dropped from the Standard Speed Test display and could cause dysfunction of the test.

3. No control characters should be included in the STDTST.001 file. Control characters are often present in word processors in the form of preset margins, double-spacing, automatic carriage returns, and other features designed to simplify word processing. These functions will not be compatible with the Typing Tutor III program and should be deactivated if necessary.

4. While typing in the test, press RETURN immediately following the last character of each line. Typing even a single space before pressing RETURN will be cause for error when taking the test.

5. Save your test on the program diskette under the name STDTST.001 (the last three characters are two zeros and a one).

Important! Read Before Opening Sealed Diskette

End User License Agreement

The software in this package is sold only on the condition that the purchaser (hereinafter referred to as "You") agrees with KRIYA SYSTEMS, INC. (hereinafter referred to as "KRIYA") and SIMON & SCHUSTER, INC. (hereinafter referred to as "S&S") to the terms and conditions set forth below. **Read this end user license agreement carefully. You will be bound by the terms of this agreement if you open the sealed diskette.** If you do not agree to the terms contained in this End User License Agreement, return the entire product, along with your receipt, to *Simon & Schuster Electronic Publishing Division, 1230 Avenue of the Americas, New York, New York, 10020, Att: Refunds,* and your purchase price will be refunded.

   KRIYA agrees to grant and you agree to accept a personal, nonexclusive license to use the software program and associated documentation in this package, or any part of it (hereinafter referred to as the "Licensed Product"), subject to the following terms and conditions:

1. *License*
   The license granted to You hereunder authorizes You to use the Licensed Product in any machine-readable form on any single computer system (hereinafter referred to as the "System"). A separate license, pursuant to a separate End User License Agreement, is required for each other computer system on which you intend to use the Licensed Product.

2. *Term*
   This End User License Agreement is effective from the date of purchase by You of the Licensed Product and shall remain in force until terminated. You may terminate this End User License Agreement at any time by destroying the Licensed Product together with all copies in any form made by You or received by You. Your right to use or copy the Licensed Product will terminate if You fail to comply with any of the terms or conditions of this End User License Agreement. You agree upon such termination to destroy the Licensed Product together with all copies in any form made by You or received by You.

3. *Restriction Against Transfer*
   This End User License Agreement, and the Licensed Product, may not be assigned, sublicensed or otherwise transferred by You to another party unless the other party agrees to accept the terms and conditions of this End User License Agreement. If You transfer the Licensed Product, You must at the same time either transfer all copies whether in printed or machine-readable form to the same party or destroy any copies not transferred.

4. *Restrictions Against Copying or Modifying the Licensed Product*
   The Licensed Product is copyrighted and may not be further copied without the prior written approval of KRIYA, except that you may make one copy for back-up purposes provided you reproduce and include the complete copyright notice on the back-up copy. Any non-authorized copying is in violation of this Agreement and may constitute a violation of the United States Copyright Law for which You could be liable in a civil or criminal suit. **You may not use, transfer, modify, copy or otherwise reproduce the licensed product, or any part of it, except as expressly permitted in this End User License Agreement.** You agree to maintain appropriate records of the location of both copies of the Licensed Product, or any part of it. The original and the copy of the Licensed Product, or any part of it, shall be the property of KRIYA.

5. *Protection and Security*
   You agree not to deliver or otherwise make available the Licensed Product or any part of it, including without limitation program listings, object code and source code, to any person other than KRIYA or its employees, except for purposes specifically related to your use of the Licensed Product, without the prior written consent of KRIYA. You agree to take all reasonable steps to safeguard the Licensed Product to ensure that no unauthorized person shall have access to it and that no unauthorized copy of any part of it in any form shall be made.

6. **Limited Warranty**
   If you are the original consumer purchaser of a diskette and it is found to be defective in materials or workmanship (which shall not include problems relating to the nature or operation of the Licensed Product) under normal use, S&S will replace it free of charge (or, at S&S's option, refund your purchase price) within 30 days following the date of purchase. Following the 30-day period, and up to one year after purchase, S&S will replace any such defective diskette upon payment of a $5 charge (or, at S&S's option, refund your purchase price), provided that the Limited Warranty Registration Card has been filed within 30 days following the date of purchase. Any request for replacement of a defective diskette must be accompanied by the original defective diskette and proof of date of purchase and purchase price. S&S shall have no obligation to replace a diskette (or refund your purchase price) based on claims of defects in the nature or operation of the Licensed Product.

Neither KRIYA, S&S nor anyone else who has been involved in the creation or production of this product makes any other express warranties regarding the diskette and makes no express warranties at all regarding the Licensed Product. Any implied warranties, of merchantability, fitness or otherwise, applicable to this product shall be limited in duration to the duration of the express warranty relating to the diskette described above, and the sole remedy for breach of any applicable warranty, express or implied, shall be replacement (or, at S&S's option, refund of purchase price) in accordance with the procedures described in the prior paragraph. Neither KRIYA, S&S nor anyone else who has been involved in the creation or production of this product shall be liable for any direct, indirect, incidental, special or consequential damages, whether arising out of the use or inability to use the product, or any breach of a warranty, and shall have no responsibility except to replace the diskette pursuant to this limited warranty (or, at its option, provide a refund of the purchase price).

Some states do not allow limitations on how long an implied warranty lasts, nor exclusions or limitations of incidental or consequential damages, so the above limitations and exclusions may not apply to You.

This warranty gives you specific legal rights, and you may also have other rights which vary from state to state.

No sales personnel or other representative of any party involved in the distribution of the Licensed Product is authorized by KRIYA or S&S to make any warranties with respect to the diskette or the Licensed Product beyond those contained in this Agreement. **Oral statements do not constitute warranties,** shall not be relied upon by You, and are not part of this Agreement. The entire agreement between KRIYA, S&S and You is embodied in this Agreement.

7. *General*

If any provision of this End User License Agreement is determined to be invalid under any applicable statute or rule of law, it shall be deemed omitted and the remaining provisions shall continue in full force and effect. This End User License Agreement is to be governed by and construed in accordance with the laws of the State of Illinois.